ART OF BIRDS

The Texas Pan American Series

Pablo Neruda

Art of Birds

translated by Jack Schmitt
with illustrations by Jack Unruh

UNIVERSITY OF TEXAS PRESS, AUSTIN

Copyright © 1985 by Herederos de Pablo Neruda
All rights reserved
Printed in the United States of America
First Edition, 1985

Translated from *Arte de pájaros*,
© Herederos de Pablo Neruda

Requests for permission to reproduce material
from this work should be sent to Permissions,
University of Texas Press, Box 7819, Austin, Texas 78713.

Library of Congress Cataloging in Publication Data
Neruda, Pablo, 1904–1973.
 Art of birds.
 (The Texas Pan American series)
 1. Birds—Poetry.   I. Schmitt, Jack, 1932–
II. Title.   III. Series.
 PQ8097.N4A8513   1985   861   84-7585
 ISBN 0-292-70371-6

The Texas Pan American Series is published
with the assistance of a revolving publication fund
established by the Pan American Sulphur Company.

JP
3/86

CONTENTS

THE BIRDS

RARAE AVES

A Letter Requesting Wood

I lost the rain and the wind
and wonder what I've gained.
Since I lost the green shade
I sometimes sink and die:
it's my heart that isn't happy
and searches beneath my shoes
for things spent or lost.
Perhaps that sad land
moves in me like a ship:
but I changed planets.

The rain no longer knows me.

PABLO NERUDA, *Extravagario*

TRANSLATOR'S INTRODUCTION

CHILE, stretching some twenty-six hundred miles from north to south, averages but a hundred miles wide. Some of the world's most arid deserts in the north and agricultural lands in the central valley give way to the pristine temperate-zone rainforest extending toward the south. Pablo Neruda (1904–1973), the Chilean Nobel laureate, was raised in Temuco, roughly two-thirds of the way southward, where farming areas yield to timberlands. The capital of Cautín Province, Temuco is also the gateway to the spectacular Chilean Lake District, which lies between the towns of Temuco and Puerto Montt. Due to the extremely heavy precipitation from the Andean ridge to the coast, the valleys, set against the magnificent backdrop of the Andes, are blessed with snowcapped volcanic mountains, glaciers, countless rivers and lakes, and a lush, dense, impenetrable vegetation, an ideal habitat for the rainforest flora and fauna. According to Neruda, these are the lands that "sank their roots into my poetry . . . My life is a long pilgrimage that is always turning on itself, always returning to the woods in the south, to the forest lost to me." It is thus fact, not nationalistic pride, that motivates Neruda to claim that "anyone who hasn't been in the Chilean forest doesn't know this planet."[1]

Emir Rodríguez-Monegal correctly asserts that the "last paradox" of Neruda, "a millionaire in books and personae, is that all his works originate and end in a single definitive image: the rain that 'a sad child like me' hears forever after."[2] In the poetry of his maturity, Neruda insistently recalls the familiar markers of his childhood: Temuco and its surroundings, summer holidays on the coast (Puerto Saavedra, Imperial del Sur), horseback trips along the beach and through the forest to Lake Budi, his dramatic escape from Chile to Argentina many years later by way of Temuco, Ranco and Maihue lakes, through the forest and over the Andes on horseback to San Martín, and his obsessive catalogs of Mapuche place-names, the flora and fauna, the entire vast, humming nature of the southern rainforest.

---

[1] *Memoirs*, translated by Hardie St. Martin (New York: Farrar, Straus and Giroux, 1977), pages 191 and 6.

[2] *El viajero inmóvil* (Caracas: Monte Avila Editores, C.A., 1977), page 12. An English translation of this study would be very useful, as it is to date the most comprehensive critical and biographical study available. In English, John Felstiner's *Translating Neruda: The Way to Macchu Picchu* (Stanford: Stanford University Press, 1980) and a more recent study by Manuel Durán and Margery Safir, *Earth Tones: The Poetry of Pablo Neruda* (Bloomington: Indiana University Press, 1981), provide a more comprehensive understanding of the life and works of Neruda. Felstiner's fascinating and convincing study successfully bridges the gap between translation and interpretative criticism.

In an interview with Robert Bly, Neruda said, "Poetry in South America is a different matter altogether. You see, there are in our countries rivers which have no names, trees nobody knows, and birds which nobody has described . . . Our duty, then, as we understand it, is to express what is unheard of. Everything has been painted in Europe. But not in America. In that sense, Whitman was a great teacher . . . He had tremendous eyes to see everything—he taught us to see things. He was our poet."[3]

To name an object is to identify and catalog it, showing how it differs from other things which superficially it may resemble. A scientific name always refers to the same plant or animal and may be used in any part of the world. It is thus significant that Neruda often gives both the Spanish and the scientific names for the flora and fauna closest to his heart, for there is just one correct scientific name for each animal or plant. In Chile, for example, the lapwing (*Vanellus* species) is known as the *queltehue*, a name of Araucanian origin. In Argentina, the same bird is called the *tero-tero*. "Everything exists in the word," says Neruda.[4]

Birds are only a small, albeit important, aspect of Neruda's multifaceted evocation of nature, and nature imagery is a constant in his poetry from early on. He had quite thoroughly covered the subject of birds before he began to write the *Art of Birds*. Among the most beautiful of his more than two hundred odes are those dedicated to the birds: "To the Birds of Chile," "To Bird-watching," "To the Oriole," "To Hummingbirds," "To the Gull," "To a Wandering Albatross," "To the Migration of Birds," "To September Wings," and "To the Gulls of Antofagasta." There are many bird poems and countless images and instances of figurative language relating to birds and flight in other books by Neruda.

Arte de pájaros was first published in 1966, with color illustrations by Nemesio Antúnez, Mario Carreño, Héctor Herrera, and Mario Toral.[5] It is a brief but beautiful, charming, loving, and playful book in which the poet's passionate lyricism and powers of observation cannot but impress the reader. Of the fifty-three poems in it, thirty-eight are devoted to the "real" birds (*pajarintos*), twelve are riddles (*pajarantes*), and three longer poems ("Migration," "The Flight," and "The Poet Says Good-bye to the Birds") give cohesion and coherence to the entire book.

---

3   "The Lamb and the Pine Cone," in *Pablo Neruda—Twenty Poems*, translated by James Wright and Robert Bly (Madison, Minn.: Sixties Press, Odin House, 1967), pages 102 to 103.

4   *Memoirs*, page 53.

5   *Arte de pájaros* (Santiago: Lord Cochrane, Ediciones Sociedad de Amigos del Arte Contemporáneo, 1966). For my translations, I used the third edition of the *Obras completas*, volume 2 (Buenos Aires: Editorial Losada, S.A., 1968), pages 673 to 720. I consulted A. W. Johnson's two-volume *The Birds of Chile and Adjacent Regions of Argentina, Bolivia and Peru* (Buenos Aires: Platt Establecimientos Gráficos, S.A., 1965) for information on the birds of Chile. Following Johnson's study, I made seventeen changes (mostly to correct typographical errors) in the scientific names given to the birds in the Spanish original of *Arte de pájaros*. After the recent publication of the sixth edition of the American Ornithologists' Union *Check-list of North American Birds* (Lawrence, Kans.: Allen Press, 1983), I made further changes in the birds' scientific and common names in order to update and correct this terminology and facilitate identification. One could expect two objections of a technical nature in the poems "American Kestrel" and "Harris' Hawk." First, it is unlikely that a kestrel could manage a "hare" or "bird" (they take small rodents, lizards, grasshoppers, etc.); second, the Harris' hawk is neither a "falcon" nor "white" (the adult is very dark).

Neruda's impressionistic sketches are brilliant in capturing movement, light, the habitat, and the peculiar characteristics of the different species. The poems reflect a broad range of moods and feelings. Birds of prey and carrion birds are presented in an ominous or negative light, and Neruda the social critic emerges in a number of the poems. Several of the most painfully nostalgic poems are those dedicated to the birds of the Far South. The large and sociable black-faced ibis is synonymous with the rainforest lakes, rivers, marshes, and meadows, and Neruda situates it in the heart of the Lake District, "from Ranco to Lake Maihue / and the meadows of Llanquihue." He sees the flying formations of ibis in a reverie, perhaps from the streets of a foreign city, where he poignantly recalls "the fluvial waters," "the forest's secret sounds," "a silence of / bursting roots and seeds," the "pungent rainforest aroma, / feet sinking in leaves, / lakes like opened eyes," and the "smell of fallen cinnamon laurel."

In his poem to the flamingo, Neruda returns to the beacons of his paradise lost: the Toltén River (just south of Temuco), "the implacable sea" (Puerto Saavedra and Imperial del Sur), "the river" (the Cautín, which flows west through Temuco to the Imperial River and the sea), "the water enclosed in the lake" (Lake Budi), the flowering ulmo (*Eucryphia cordifolia*, heartleaf eucryphia), which in summer blankets the south with clouds of fragrant white flowers. The ubiquitous chucao tapaculo, a bird of both good and bad omen that is always heard but seldom seen in the rainforest, is situated "in the entangled dampness / of the Gulf of Reloncaví."

The elegant black-necked swan, perhaps the most important bird to the poet, receives the shortest (two mysterious lines) poem in the book. In one of the first chapters of his *Memoirs*, Neruda gives a moving account of his attempts to revive an injured swan that had been brought to him from Lake Budi to Puerto Saavedra. After twenty days of nursing it, he was carrying it back home from the river when he "felt a ribbon unrolling, and something like a black arm brushed my face. It was the long, sinuous neck falling. That's when I learned that swans don't sing when they die."[6] A beautiful evocation of these swans in Lake Budi appears in his poem "El lago de los cisnes" ("Swan Lake").[7] The poem on the Chilean pigeon, which is found in the heart of the forest, particularly in stands of araucaria pines, is unusually tender and poignant. This bird was attacked by Newcastle disease in the mid fifties and its numbers so reduced that it seemed doomed to extinction. Full protection of the species has fortunately resulted in its slow comeback.

Perhaps some words about this translation are in order. I received a sabbatical grant for research on Brazilian literature during the 1981 spring semester. I had planned a fly-fishing trip through the virgin trout waters of southern Chile and Argentina en route to Brazil. Pablo Neruda's works were initially a side trip to my Chilean adventure, starting with a reading of his *Memoirs*, which in turn moti-

6   "My First Poem," in *Memoirs*, pages 18 to 19.
7   *Isla Negra: A Notebook*, translated by Alastair Reid (New York: Farrar, Straus and Giroux, 1981), pages 40 to 43. Thanks to Alastair Reid and his many fine translations of Neruda's works in recent years, a better knowledge and understanding of the works and poetic characteristics of the great Chilean poet have been made available to an ever larger Anglo-American readership.

vated a chronological study of his complete works. His evocation of the Far South inspired a study of the Lake District flora and fauna and an etymological study of Mapuche, inasmuch as most of the place-names and many of the names of Lake District flora and fauna are derived from this Araucanian Indian language. Then, with a backpack and camera equipment, I traveled south of Temuco to the eastern side of Lake Panguipulli and the remote Andean ridge, which I followed south, mostly on foot and horseback, for approximately five hundred miles. My trip included most of the familiar markers evoked in Neruda's poetry "from Ranco to Lake Maihue / and the meadows of Llanquihue," plus a long roadless (at the time) stretch south of Puerto Montt, between Chaitén and Coyhaique. I placed my destiny in the hands of noble and generous strangers, mostly dirt farmers, in that lost corner of the globe. By the time I entered Andean Patagonia, in far south Argentina, I had explored the uttermost part of the earth under the impress of a visionary poet's writings and experienced the adventure of a lifetime. I was constantly aware of the birds. And the act of translating the *Arte de pájaros* has helped me recapture part of that adventure.

A couple of closing comments before allowing the birds to speak for themselves. Out of fairness to Argentina, it should be stressed that the Lake District, most of the birds, even some of the lakes are shared by these two beautiful countries and peoples. In the Argentine provinces of Neuquén, Río Negro, and Chubut, Andean Patagonia lies in the shadow of the Chilean rainforest and the birds move freely from country to country without visas, passports, work permits, or border inspections. I know Pablo Neruda always supported such freedom of movement for the peoples of this planet as well as the birds. Finally, I shall confess that these translations have been a labor of love, and I should like to thank the great Chilean poet for his generous legacy of beauty and love, his reverence for life, his plea for justice and equality, peace and goodwill, and his passionate commitment to the human enterprise.

EDITOR'S NOTE: In order to accommodate the newly commissioned illustrations, the order of the poems has been altered on pages 29–30 and 57–58.

ART OF BIRDS

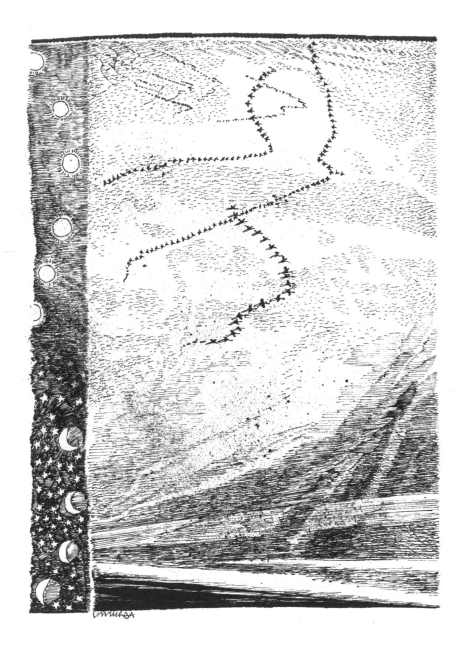

MIGRATION

All day, column after column,
a squadron of feathers,
a fluttering airborne
ship
crossed
the tiny infinity
of the window where I search,
question, work, observe, wait.

The tower of sand
and marine space
join there, comprise
song, movement.

Above, the sky unfolds.

So it was: palpitating,
sharp right angles passed
heading northward, westward,
toward open space,
toward the star,
toward the spire of salt and solitude
where the sea casts its clocks to the winds.

It was an angle of birds
steering for
that latitude of iron and snow,
inexorably advancing along
their rectilinear road:
the skyborne numbers
flew with the hungry rectitude
of a well-aimed arrow, winging
their way to procreate, formed
by urgent love and geometry.

I kept looking as far as
the eye could see and saw

nothing but orderly flight,
the multitude of wings against the wind:
I saw serenity multiplied
in that transparent hemisphere
crossed by the obscure decision
of those birds in the firmament.

I saw only the flyway.

All remained celestial.

But among the throngs of birds
homing for their destination
flock after flock sketched out
triangular
victories
united by the voice of a single flight,
by the unity of fire,
by blood,
by thirst, by hunger,
by the cold,
by the precarious day that wept
before being swallowed by night,
by the erotic urgency of life:
the unity of birds
flew
toward the toothless black coasts,
lifeless pinnacles, yellow isles,
where the sun works overtime
and the plural pavilion of sardines
spreads over the warm sea.

On the stone assaulted
by the birds
the secret was set forth:
stone, moisture, excrement, and solitude
will ferment and beneath the blood-red sun
sandy offspring will be born

and they, too, will one day fly back
to the tempestuous cold light,
to the antarctic feet of Chile.

Now they pass, filling the distance,
a faint flapping of wings against the light,
a throbbing winged unity

that flies without breaking

from the migratory

body

which ashore divides,
disperses.

Above the water, in the sky,
the innumerable bird flies on,
the vessel is one,
the transparent ship
builds unity with so many wings,
with so many eyes opened to the sea,
sails over a singular peacefulness
with the movement of one immense wing.

Seabird, migratory foam,
wing from north and south, wave wing,
cluster deployed by flight,
multiplied hungry heart,
you will arrive, great bird, to strip
from the necklace the fragile eggs to be
hatched by the wind and nourished by the sand
until another flight again
multiplies life, death, growth,
wet cries, hot dung,
being born again, and leaving, far
from the windy waste to another windy waste.

Far
from that silence, flee, polar birds,
to the vast rocky silence
and from the nest to the errant number,
sea arrows, bequeath me
the wet glory of time elapsed,
the renowned permanence of feathers
that are born, that die, endure, and throb,
creating fish by fish their long sword,
cruelty against cruelty, the very light
and against the wind and the sea, life.

THE BIRDS

WANDERING ALBATROSS
Diomedea exulans

The wind sails the open sea
steered by the albatross
that glides, falls, dances, climbs,
hangs motionless in the fading light,
touches the waves' towers,
settles down in
the disorderly element's
seething mortar
while the salt crowns it with laurels
and the furious foam hisses,
skims the waves
with its great symphonic wings,
leaving above the tempest
a book that flies on forever:
the statute of the wind.

**BLACK-CHESTED
BUZZARD-EAGLE**
Geranoaetus melanoleucus

Bitter bird, cold eagle,
sword of the cordilleras,
motionless in your eternity,
in the indifferent years,
in the stone of agony.

Harsh-plumed eagle,
I know your black language,
your cyclones' menace,
your bloodthirsty transparency,
your death-stained talons,
and I know you return defeated
to your mountains of stone and snow,
to the Andes' great silence,
to the tower of thorns.

The rose kept flowering,
the spring again spoke
its crystal conversation:
the new nests were filled
by springtime's command,
the hare stretched out on the moss
to give birth at twilight:
the clarity of the moon, of the stars,
flowed like rivers in an estuary
and you there alone, awake,
not being born or flowering—
alone with the night.

PERUVIAN PELICAN
Pelecanus thagus

Seated upon the sea the pelican
ponders profound problems:
the ocean's capacity
to provide nourishment,
the repetition of waves,
the whale's solitude,
the moon's sorceries,
the wind's coordinates.

Impassive judge of the sea:
time rolls over its skull
and a drop of wave or rain
runs down its long nose
like a transparent dictum.

Rocked by the surf like a nest
or an abandoned cradle,
the pelican measures
the consumed fish that accumulate,
like plastic money, in the purse
hanging from its mandible.

Schools of sardines,
pale autumn fish,
smooth hake from Taitao,
knife-colored yellowjacks,
even phosphorescent mollusks,
tentacles, satanic squid, and
urticarial cephalopods are stashed
in the pelican's purse.

Suddenly the miser lifts
its fish-laden pouch,
extends two lead wings,
the iron plumage takes to the air
and cruises the silence in silence
like a sacred ship.

**BLACK-FACED
IBIS**
Theristicus melanopis

I know the fluvial waters,
and from so much loving water and soil
the forest's secret sounds
have become such a part of me
that I sometimes go walking
with so many birds,
with such a silence of
bursting roots and seeds,
that when I fall asleep I keep
reliving that sonorous silence,
but I awaken or am awakened by
the large, languorous black-faced ibis
that lingered in my dream
with their aluminum trumpets.

From Ranco to Lake Maihue
and the meadows of Llanquihue
the regiments of metallic ibis
travel in formation:
suddenly they entered my dream
like a flight of white furniture:
wings beating in slow motion,
somnambulistic southern love,
pungent rainforest aroma,
feet sinking in leaves,
lakes like opened eyes
penetrating the foliage,
smell of fallen cinnamon laurel,
smell of time and moisture.

I awakened in the middle of the street:
the birds from the Far South flew on,
ringing out in the wind.

AMERICAN
KESTREL
Falco sparverius

High noon opened up:
the sun in the center, crowned.
The earth awaited indecisively
some movement in the sky
and everyone remained
indecipherably still.

At that slender second
the hawk hammered its flight,
cut loose from the firmament,
and swooped like a sudden shiver.

The landscape remained serene
and the woodlands were not frightened,
the volcanoes were still aloof,
the river kept proclaiming
its abrupt and wet lineage:
everything kept throbbing
in that green-patterned pause
except a hare, a bird,
something that flew or ran,
something that used to live
on that blood-spattered spot.

**BLACK-NECKED
SWAN**

Cygnus melanocoryphus

Above the swimming snow
a long black question mark.

CALIFORNIA QUAIL
Callipepla californica

Between Yumbel and Cuatro Trigos
I saw a shadow, a shape, a bird
slipping away with its beauty,
a fruit, a feathered flower,
a bird of pure pear,
a circumstance of the air,
a sandy smoky egg:
I approached—called out, its eyes
shone with the hostile rectitude
of two flaming lances
and above its pride it wore
two plumes like two banners:
I had no sooner seen
that vision than it vanished
and I was left with the dusk,
with the smoke, the haze, and the night,
with the solitude of the road.

GUANAY
CORMORANT
Phalacrocorax
bougainvillii

Crucified on the rock,
the motionless black-coated cross
stubbornly posed in twisted profile.
The sun fell on the coastal stones
like a galloping horse:
its shoes unleashed
a million furious sparks,
a million seadrops,
and the crucified steering wheel
did not blink on the cross:
the surf swelled up and gave birth:
the stone trembled in delivery:
the foam whispered softly:
and there, like a hanged Negro,
the cormorant remained dead,
the cormorant remained alive,
remained alive and dead and cross
with its stiff black wings
opened above the water:
remained like a cruel gaffing hook
plunged into the rock's salt
and from so many angry blows,
from so much green and fire and fury,
from the forces gathered
along the howling seacoast
it looked like a menace:
it was the cross and the gallows:
the night nailed to the cross,
the agony of darkness: but
suddenly it fled to the sky,
flew like a black arrow,
and climbed in cyclical form
with its snowy black suit,
with a star's or ship's repose.
And above the unruly ocean—
a gnashing of sea and cold—
it flew flew flew flew
its pure equation in space.

ANDEAN
CONDOR
Vultur gryphus

In its iron coffin it dwells
among the rusty stones
feeding on horseshoes.

In the mountains the north wind
whistles and howls like a missile
and the condor leaves its casket,
sharpens its talons on the rocks,
spreads its mystical plumage,
flies to the end of the sky,
gallops the concave heights
with its iron wings,
and pecks at the sky's zinc,
waiting for a sign of blood:
a motionless speck,
the heartbeat that prepares
to die and be devoured.

The black cyclone planes down
and falls like a cruel fist:
death waited down below.

Above, cruel cordilleras,
like bloodstained cacti,
and the bitter-colored sky.
It soars back to its dwelling,
folds its imperious wings
and again stretches out to sleep
in its abominable coffin.

HOUSE WREN
Troglodytes aedon

Little round neighbor, all
dressed up in feathered finery,
always after your treasure:
hunting for a stray atom,
a notion, a filament,
a trifle in the brambles,
an eyelid in the underbrush:
something surely there because
a wren turns upside down and inside out:
its agile eyes sparkle,
its tiny tail cocked
straight toward the clouds,
it comes and goes and then returns,
suddenly chirps, vanishes from sight
until it explodes again
from its feather-colored nest,
leaving behind its minute eggs,
round little works of wonder
from which a wren's curiosity
will eventually pop out
to investigate springtime.

RUFOUS-
COLLARED
SPARROW
Zonotrichia capensis

You awakened me yesterday, friend,
and I went out to meet you:
the universe smelled of clover,
of a star opened in the dew:
who are you, and why were you singing
so intimately sonorous,
so uselessly precise?

Why did the fountain flow
with your trill's precision,
a drop of water's clock,
your fragrant little violin
questioning the plums,
the indifferent headspring,
the color of lizards,
asking pure questions
that no one can answer?

I had no sooner seen you, passerby,
minuscule musician, fresh
daybreak's tenor, proprietor
of morning purity, than I
understood you were bringing back
with your little water flute
so many things that had died:
so many petals buried
beneath the smokestacks,
the smog, and the pavement.
Your crystal performance
brings us back to the dew.

GRASSLAND
YELLOW-FINCH
Sicalis luteola

It's beyond doubt, between
sky and leaves the green will stay on,
the trill will continue to trill:
the sonorous messenger arrived,
arrived dropping
its tiny yellow weight
like a lemon shedding dew
between body and wing,
the errant water that sings,
the melodious circumstances.

It planed down through the air
and sputtered out its trill
as if it were flying on fire,
as if its flight down
were held up by the music.

It seems as if it had fallen
from the branch enveloped in pollen
and had perfumed the air
that kept reverberating
when it trilled its delirium
and its crystal news.

**SLENDER-
BILLED
PARAKEET**
*Enicognathus
leptorhynchus*

The tree had so many leaves
it was toppling with treasure,
from so much green it blinked
and never closed its eyes.

That's no way to sleep.

But the fluttering foliage
went flying off green and alive,
each bud learned to fly,
and the tree was left naked,
weeping in the winter rain.

CHUCAO
TAPACULO
Scelorchilus rubecula

Oh, what a cry in the wilderness!

I walk the woods, broad leaves,
raindrops, cantharides,
and my feet sink in the ground
as in a soaking sponge:
the shade I cross is cold,
cold the silence and transparent:
no one passes this way,
on this side of the earth,
through these pages of the water:
no lost travelers
or horses, just the forest,
the mountain's emanation:
its crushed tresses:
its infinite green eyes:
and the chucao launches its lance,
its long bubbling call:
the watery cry shatters
a thousand long years of silence
when there were only falling leaves
and the roots occupied
this kingdom like invaders.

Errant, high-pitched sadness,
song, bell of the wilderness,
the chucao's obscure arrow,
the only supernatural trill
in the entangled dampness
of the Gulf of Reloncaví.

COMMON
DIUCA-FINCH
Diuca diuca

Off to mass in her mantle
goes the sweet prim thing,
goes in her dashing dress,
perfectly gray and white,
perfectly tidy and bright,
flies well groomed and attired
to avoid wrinkling the sky,
has much to do:
inspect the poppies,
direct the cruel bees,
interrogate the dew,
until she picks up her guitar
and starts to trill to trill.

CHILEAN
FLAMINGO
Phoenicopterus chilensis

I, Pablo Neruda, was a child,
neighbor of the water in Toltén,
of the implacable sea, the river,
of the water enclosed in the lake.

The dense fragrant forest
was photographed in the waters
and the double ulmo tree flowered
above the forest and in the water.

Then, oh, then I lived,
honor of transparent time,
the vision of a roseate angel
that winged by in slow motion.

Its body was made of feathers,
its wings were petals,
it was a flying rose
swinging toward sweetness.

The angel settled into the water
like a ship of mother-of-pearl
and its pink rosebush neck
glistened in the light.

I abandoned those regions,
dressed in tails and iron,
changed languages and stature,
resurrected from many deaths,
was bitten by much sorrow,
kept changing one happiness
for another,
but deep down within me,
like in that lost lake,
lives the vision of a bird
or an indelible angel
that transformed the day's light
with its splendorous being
and its rosy movement.

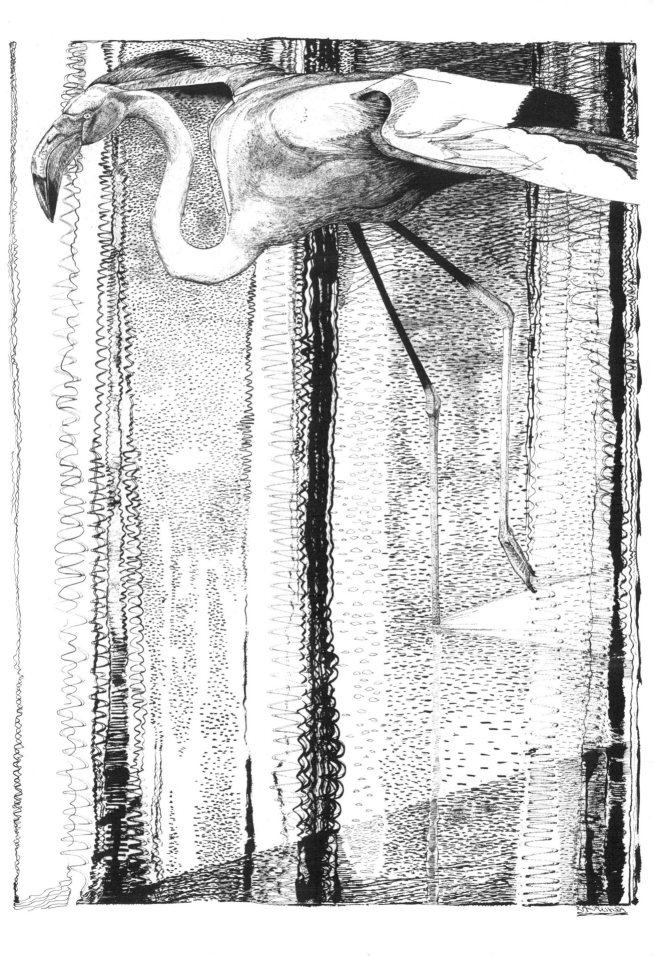

GREAT EGRET
Casmerodius albus

The motionless snow has two
long legs in the lagoon,
the white silk has one
body of fishing snow.

Why is it so immersed in thought?

Why on just one leg
does it wait for a snowy spouse?

Why does it sleep standing in the water?

Does it sleep with its eyes open?

When does it shut its white eyes?

Why in the devil is your name egret?

GRAY GULL
Larus modestus

The gull adroitly opened,
in seafoam and stupor,
two wandering pointers,
kept stationary with
two wings stretched out in the sky,
two shining secretaries of the light,
until it flew off, however,
to the east and to the west,
to the north and to the snow,
to the Moon and to the Sun.

BLUE-AND-
WHITE
SWALLOW
Pygochelidon
cyanoleuca

The returning swallow
brought me a blank letter,
a letter written with air,
with springtime mist:
it streaked back and forth,
threatening the minutes
with its velvety virtue
and its darting flight.

In fact it has returned
to Isla Negra's seafroth,
dancing in the ocean sky
as though it were home,
dropping from the sky
a premature fragrance
with the news it brought me
in a transparent letter.

BLACK-
CHINNED
SISKIN
Spinus barbatus

A little yellow god
passed between the poplars—
flew fast as the wind
and left on high a tremor,
a flute of pure stone,
a thread of vertical water,
springtime's violin:
like a feather in the wind
it passed, tiny little thing,
the day's pulse, dust, pollen,
nothing perhaps, yet the light,
the day, the gold kept quivering.

| 44 | BLACK VULTURE | The vulture opened its Parish, |
| | *Coragyps atratus* | endorsed its black habits, |

44   **BLACK**
        VULTURE
        Coragyps atratus

The vulture opened its Parish,
endorsed its black habits,
flew about in search of sinners,
diminutive crimes, robberies,
lamentable cattle thefts,
inspecting everything from above:
fields, homes, dogs, sand,
it sees everything without looking,
flies outstretched, opening
its priestly garb to the sun.

The vulture, God's spy,
does not smile at springtime:
it circles round and round, measuring heaven,
solemnly settles on the ground,
and folds up like an umbrella.

RED-BREASTED MEADOWLARK
Pezites militaris

Why show me every day
your bloody heart?

What crime is on your chest,
what indelible kiss of blood,
what hunter's shot?

Why do you rush and search and burn
with that bright red breast,
looking without haste and without fear,
looking at man with your eyes?

If you're looking for a judge,
why do you slip away
with cold eyes and abrupt wings
to another signpost where
your heart glitters again
in the bloody sun?

RINGED
KINGFISHER
Ceryle torquata

King looked from its branch
and Fisher submerged,
Kingfisher dove down
and Kingfisher fished,
King dove down, poor bird,
and Fisher surfaced rich
with its load of live silver
and some blue drops of water,
because the fisher King
feeds only on rainbows,
on light rippling in the water:
then sits down and consumes
its catch of quivering fish.

MAGELLANIC
WOODPECKER
Campephilus
magellanicus

The woodpecker toco toc:
under the sun the forests distill
water, resin, night, honey,
the hazelnut trees don
galloons of scarlet pomp:
the burned logs bleed on,
the foxes of Boroa are asleep,
the leaves grow silently
while the roots' language
circulates beneath the ground:
suddenly in the green silence
the woodpecker toco toc.

INTERLUDE:
THE FLIGHT

Hands shading eyes,
I follow the high flight:
honoring heaven, the bird
traverses
the transparency, without soiling the day.

Winging westward, it climbs
each step up to the naked blue:
the entire sky is its tower,
and the world is cleansed by its movement.

Though the violent bird
seeks blood in the rose of space,
its structure is
arrow and flower in flight,
and in the light its wings
are fused with air and purity.

O feathers destined
not to tree, meadow, or combat,
or to the atrocious ground
or sweatshop,
but to the conquest
of a transparent fruit!

I celebrate the skydance
of gulls and petrels
attired in snow
as though I had
a standing invitation:
I participate
in their velocity and repose,
in the pause and haste of snow.

What flies in me is manifest
in the errant equation of those wings.

O wind aside the black condor's
iron flight in the mist!
Whistling wind that transposed
the hero's murderous scimitar:
you receive the harsh flight's blow
like a coat of armor plate,
repeat its menace in the sky
until all becomes blue again.

The flight of a dart,
every swallow's mission,
flight of the nightingale and its sonata,
the cockatoo and its showy crest.

Hummingbirds flying in a looking glass
stir sparkling emeralds,
and flying through the dew
the partridge shakes
the mint's green soul.

I, who learned to fly with every flight
of pure professors
in the woods, at sea, in the ravines,
on my back in the sand,
or in dreams,
remained here, tied
to the roots,
to the magnetic mother, the earth,
lying to myself
and flying
only within,
alone and in the dark.

A plant dies and is buried again,
man's feet return to the terrain,
only wings evade death.

The world is a crystal sphere,
if he does not fly man loses his way—
cannot understand transparency.
That is why I profess
unconfined clarity
and from the birds I learned
passionate hope,
the certainty and truth of flight.

CHILEAN
TINAMOU
Nothoprocta perdicaria

Exhalation! It ran, flew,
skated off with wings whirring,
and the aroma kept quivering
at the edge of the ravine,
the dew kept quivering,
the somnolent cereal;
while grooming, the morning
lost a flower from its diadem:
the Sunday smelled of manure
and with every sudden shot,
with every cry from the gunpowder,
the sky stopped blinking.

But, perhaps, from the roots,
from the ground, the partridge flushed,
and its crisp wings snapped:
its perfume flew past
like the ravine's soul:
a kiss of mist and moss,
a brushy movement,
the topa topa flashed
its yellow gifts
in the blue air, the partridge
lost its powdery plumage
and turned into blue air.

HARRIS' HAWK
Parabuteo unicinctus

I saw a white falcon suspended
from the sky as if by a thread,
but there was no thread:
the white falcon fluttered,

its movement was snowy,
its great wings flapped,
inside it the fire leapt
like a consuming bonfire:
hunger sharpened the steel,
the black cyclone of its talons:
it prepared the blind blood
to plunge like a stone:
terror terror its snowy light,
terror its ravenous peace.

GREEN-BACKED
FIRECROWN
Sephanoides sephanoides

I

The fire escaped and was carried
by a golden movement
that kept it hovering,
fleeting, still, tremulous:
erectile vibration, metal:
a petal from the meteors.

It flew on without flying,
focusing the diminutive sun
on a honey helicopter,
on a syllable from the emerald
that from flower to flower
disseminates the rainbow's identity.

In the sun the sunflower shakes
the sumptuous sumptuary silk
of two invisible wings,
and the most minuscule lightning
burns in pure incandescence,
static and vertiginous.

GREEN-BACKED
FIRECROWN
Sephanoides sephanoides

II

The hummingbird of seven lights,
the hummingbird of seven flowers,
looks for a thimble to live in:
its love life is hapless
without a home to go to,
far from the world and the flowers.

Your love is unlawful, sir,
come another day at another time:
the hummingbird must marry
to be able to live with his hummer:
I shall not rent you this thimble
for this unlawful traffic.

Hummingbird flew off at last
to the garden with his love,
and there came a ferocious cat
to eat the two of them up:
the hummingbird of seven flowers,
his hummer of seven colors:
the infernal cat gobbled them down
but their death was lawful.

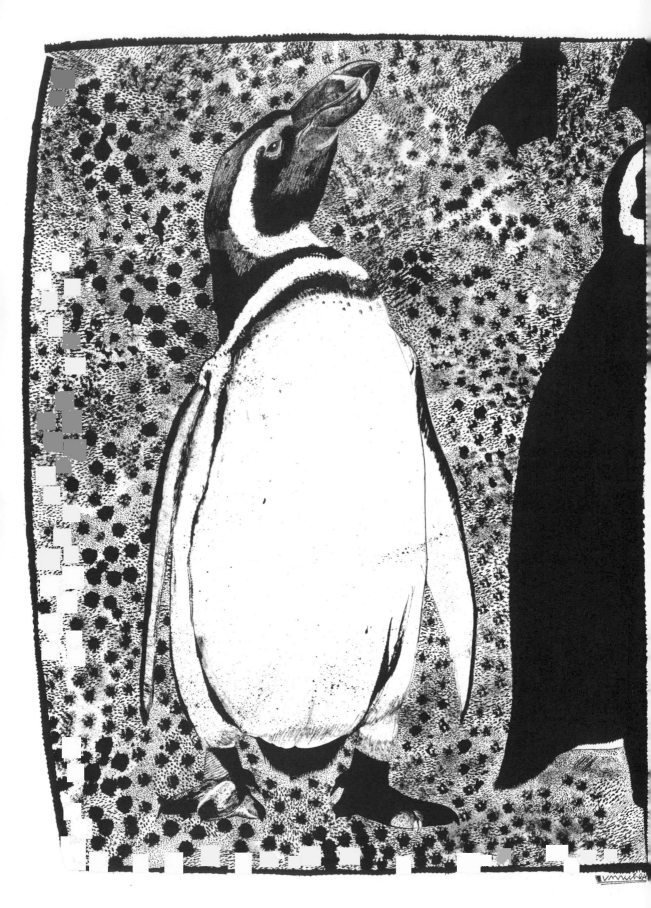

MAGELLANIC
PENGUIN
Spheniscus magellanicus

Neither clown nor child nor black
nor white but vertical
and a questioning innocence
dressed in night and snow.
The mother smiles at the sailor,
the fisherman at the astronaut,
but the child child does not smile
when he looks at the bird child,
and from the disorderly ocean
the immaculate passenger
emerges in snowy mourning.

I was without doubt the child bird
there in the cold archipelagoes
when it looked at me with its eyes,
with its ancient ocean eyes:
it had neither arms nor wings
but hard little oars
on its sides:
it was as old as the salt,
the age of moving water,
and it looked at me from its age:
since then I know I do not exist,
I am a worm in the sand.

The reasons for my respect
remained in the sand:
that religious bird
did not need to fly,
did not need to sing,
and though its form was visible
its wild soul bled salt
as if a vein from the bitter sea
had been broken.

Penguin, static traveler,
deliberate priest of the cold,
I salute your vertical salt
and envy your plumed pride.

PLUMBEOUS
RAIL
Rallus (*Ortygonax*)
sanguinolentus

The rail slipped through the shadow
to the rail's shade: it whistled,
and the afternoon became shadow,
summoned by the rail that
slipped away like a shade,
giving a watery whistle,
and the rail was seen darting
between the shadow and its whistle:
the rail's scimitar,
the indistinct shady feathers:
something flashed by with the rail,
a shadowy feather or shrill water,
the rail's forked thunderbolt,
a shadow ran to the brush,
from the brush a shadow emerged:
the rail's shadow whistled.

CHILEAN
LAPWING
Vanellus chilensis

The lapwing flew off flashing
white snow and black snow
and opened its suit
in broad daylight,
in broad morning silver:
its nuptial wings' fan was priceless:
precious the body adorned
by the morning and the plumage.

The velvety bird's
wild extravagance shone
upon the stones of Isla Negra
and I thought: where is it going?

What celestial reception?

What golden water wedding?

What salon of pure purple
among columns of hyacinths,
where only the well-dressed clouds
may accompany it?

Well, I said, perhaps it's going
to crown the tresses
of Pedro Espinosa's friend,
the naiad of the River Genil.

The diviner did no such thing:
it planed down to land
among clumps of stubble
in a fallow wheat field,
and there it launched its language,
its piercing tero tero,
while it pecked, picked,
and dispassionately devoured
a simple earthworm.

MANY-COLORED
RUSH-TYRANT
Tachuris rubrigastra

In the lagoon the cattail,
the wet reedbed,
some drops alive and aflame:
suddenly a movement,
a minuscule banner,
a scale of the rainbow:
the sun swiftly set it afire.
How were its seven colors combined?
How did it assume all the light?

There it was but was not:
the gust of wind is gone,
perhaps does not exist,
but the cattail is still quivering.

62   WHITE-
      THROATED
      TAPACULO
      Scelorchilus albicollis

It pops up hopping about the stones
above the parched grass
and pick pick pecks:
with a quick rap it dropped
its round eyes, the beak
a yellow lightning bolt.
And it changed the landscape:
its long vertical tail,
the recalcitrant feathers
pointing at high noon
raised above its rump.

CHILEAN
MOCKINGBIRD
Mimus thenca

The long-tailed mockingbird flew
dressed like scissors:
perched on a thread, it listened to
the telegraph's deep voice,
the wire's blue pulse,
heard words, kisses, numbers,
fleet petals from the soul,
then launched its trill,
released a transparent stream,
and scattered its delirium to the winds.

Mockingbird, I did not learn your lesson
of flight and song and thought:
I learned it all from the mist,
the moisture, the silence.
I did not know how to dance and fly
above the peumo trees' beauty,
submerge my soul in the boldu trees,
while away time whistling in the wind.
I did not know about your wisdom,
the speed of your trill,
the republic of your song.

I swear I'll learn whatever you profess:
to know how to fly like an arrow,
to study the secret syllables
of the outdoors and leaves,
to sing with the water and the land,
and to establish in the silence
a crystalline chair of learning.

64 **CHIMANGO
CARACARA**
Milvago chimango

Unacceptable, necessary,
insolent bird, inspector
embalmed before death,
dry caracara, feather duster,
caracara waiting for the funeral,
caracara indecisive in the rubbish,
impartial, conspicuous,
old skyhorse,
torn pants on a tile roof,
dilapidated flier,
pile of irritating feathers,
clothes hanger rusted in the urine
of an abandoned village,
beneficent caracara fallen
and raised from the dirt,
soiled by clouds of dust
until your will became faded out:
from so much scavenging about
you have no more color
than a cluster without grapes,
than a bean skin,
than hospital hair,
than buried feathers.

CHILEAN
PIGEON
Columba araucana

In my childhood I adored
the pigeon's red feet:
those red leather feet
and scarlet toes.
From what world of feathers and dreams,
from what inaccessible wardrobe,
was falconry tossed
toward my humble station?

Toward my humble station,
a hunter without a shotgun,
lost in the rain and the leaves:
the innumerable pigeons
flew down from the trees,
eating black seeds,
the forest's secret bread,
the harsh summer's berries,
consuming the sky's grain,
the ravine's expanse,
the cereal daybreak,
the dawn's delicacies.

And now they flew down to me.

They were my wild family.

They came attired in wind
and in each feather glistened
the clay's ocher veins,
the hues of the hills:
they wore the rustic poncho
of my birthright.

Farewell, pigeons, redolent
of dust, powder, and pollen:
I no longer know where those
red leather feet perched:
the wings, the cinnamon laurels'
multitudes have disappeared,
and now my family has fled
from the trees of those forests:
no one is waiting to fly for me.

It seems that only
some burned trees subsist.

AUSTRAL
BLACKBIRD
Curaeus curaeus

Whoever looks at me face to face
I shall kill with two knives,
with two furious lightning bolts:
with two icy black eyes.

I was not born for captivity.

I have a wild army,
a militant militia,
a battalion of black bullets:
no seeded field can withstand.

I fly, devour, screech, and move on,
rise and fall with a thousand wings:
nothing can stop my determination,
the black order of my feathers.

My soul is a burned log,
my plumage pure coal:
my soul and suit are black:
that's why I dance in the white sky.

I am the Black Floridor.

AUSTRAL
THRUSH
Turdus falcklandii

The thrush assured in the garden,
sure-footed, sure-eyed,
hears earthworms
squirming underground,
wears yellow leather boots
like a gentleman,
does not need to raise
its dew-laden wings
or its peppery plumage,
travels over land and grass,
traverses Chile's perfume,
the smell of dry wheat fields,
the shade of oranges,
the mint's green air,
and when it feels overwhelmed
by so many natural gifts
the melancholy thrush sighs,
takes the sadness to its wings
with its vegetable guitar,
and cries with a watery voice,
sings its liquid song
like a drop or a grape
or a quivering dart:
then the thrush is off again,
gently treading
Chile's fragrant body.

RARAE AVES

MOONCRACKER

Columba planetaris sun

Its lament reverberated
in paludal Oceania, and it
climbed with the waning night
like a metal spike
until it struck the vault,
the moon's aluminum,
and the planet was heard rending
with the extra-remote sound
of a falling ring:
it was the moon weeping.

OCTOBRINE

Primavera solstitii

The tricolored octobrine
is born, lives, and dies in October:
it has a revolver's blue shape,
feathers descended from mother-of-pearl,
tail like a celestial sign,
and this bird is fragrant
like the bee's homeland:
it sings seven copper notes:
then seven silver notes:
then seven notes of rain.

And the intense octobrine dies
a blue and natural death.

HIEROGLYPHIC BIRD
Tordus alphabeticus

Interbred to the last feather,
the labyrinthine, the amphibian
bird of enigmas
extends its sphere of action.

It jumps only in the quiet jungle,
devouring letters and numbers,
catechisms and palinodes,
magic root soups.
It strikes the star, is
terrified on everyone's turf,
enclouded in the nebulous cloud,
drenched and drowned in the water,
and in its disheveled plumage
as in its disjointed song
are shuffled faraway feathers
that looked unfathomable,
remote syllables, secrets,
colors opened suddenly
like provinces discovered
by some blind explorer,
until the dark bird assumes
by the sandy shores
the tenacious hieroglyphs
that transpire there, jingling
between the wind that combats them
and the black water's kiss.

ROSESCRATCHER

Rosacea luminica

With three claws it scratches the gold,
the saffron, and the softness
of the lofty rose-red rose,
empress of the rosebush:
it centrifugally unfurls
three wings like three sails
and sails off to the south,
preceded by the aroma
of many satiny roses.

COROLLARY
BIRD

Minus cothapa

From so much seeing and not seeing
the corollary bird
I learned that yes it knew,
I learned that no it doesn't fly,
I learned that it was on its branch,
perched on its parashade,
watching for the cyclones
that fall upon the Amazon:
its song's rumbling echo
is distributed equally
between the black Orinoco
and our torrential Acario.

Its song falls over the buzzing
of recalcitrant flies
the size of eggplants,
falls over the green vapor
that rises from the river,
over the explorers
who jot down the time,
the corollary bird's name,
the circumstances of its song.

And tumbling down the ravine
its raucous syllables grow louder,
until the bird burns out
so that Brazil can sleep.

TIUMBA
Petrosina vulnerabilis

The tiny tiumba pecks at the glass
until it perforates the windows
and enters by night to spy on
the lethargy of the naked.

It pecks into the dreams,
grinding glass and oats,
drinks the dreams' water,
catches fire in the smoldering ash,
crosses the vespertine swarms,
floats in Night's river,
and when the slumberer awakens
the tiumba keeps being a dream.

**GREATER
TINKLER**
Jorgesius saniversus

The tinkler arrived at the shore
and taking a drink in the long water
it dropped its blue tail
until the river sang,
its tail sang with the water.

The tinkler is transparent,
cannot be seen against the crystals,
and is invisible when it flies:
it is a bubble of the wind,
it is an icy fugue,
it is a crystal palpitation.

I was able to see, in white winter,
in the forsaken regions
of Aysén, remote and rainy,
a migratory flock
returning from the Glacier.

The tinklers, frightened
by the rain's furor,
drummed their icy flight
against the ship's prow
and shattered to splinters,
to transparent pieces
that falling to the water
hissed like seawater
churned to a froth by the wind.

DODOBIRD
Autoritarius miliformis

The dodobird, seated,
sensed that it didn't know it,
that it didn't fly and didn't fly
but gave out flight orders
and kept explaining wing by wing
what would happen in the atmosphere:
it made pronouncements about feathers,
revealed the sky and its currents.

The dodobird was born seated.

This sad featherless bird
grew up seated and never had
wings or song or flight.

But the dictator dictated.

It dictated the air, hope,
the sums of coming and going.

And if the matter at hand was lofty,
the dodobird was born above,
it pointed out the skyways,
it would ascend sometime,
but it was now concerned
with numbers, proprieties,
best not fly now:
"Meanwhile, you may fly."
The ferocious dodobird
sits down on its fangs
and spies on others flying:
"Not one bee will fly here
unless I so decree."

And thus the dodobird flies
but does not fly from its chair.

SHEBIRD
Matildina silvestre

With my little terrestrial bird,
my rustic earthen jug,
I break out singing
the guitar's rain:
alleged autumn arrives
like a load of firewood,
decanting the aroma
that flew through the mountains,
and grape by grape my kisses
were joined to her bunch.

This proves that the afternoon
accumulated sweetness
like the amber process
or the order of violets.

Come flying, passenger,
let's fly with the coals,
live or cold,
with the disorderly darkness
of the obscure and the ardent.

Let's enter the ash,
let's move with the smoke,
let's live by the fire.

In mid autumn
we'll set the table
over the grassy hillside,
flying over Chillán
with your guitar in your wings.

MEBIRD

Pablo insulidae nigra

I am the Pablo Bird,
bird of a single feather,
a flier in the clear shadow
and obscure clarity,
my wings are unseen,
my ears resound
when I walk among the trees
or beneath the tombstones
like an unlucky umbrella
or a naked sword,
stretched like a bow
or round like a grape,
I fly on and on not knowing,
wounded in the dark night,
who is waiting for me,
who does not want my song,
who desires my death,
who will not know I'm arriving
and will not come to subdue me,
to bleed me, to twist me,
or to kiss my clothes,
torn by the shrieking wind.

That's why I come and go,
fly and don't fly but sing:
I am the furious bird
of the calm storm.

THE POET SAYS GOOD-BYE TO THE BIRDS

A provincial poet
and birder,
I come and go about the world,
unarmed,
just whistle my way along,
submit
to the sun and its certainty,
to the rain's violin voice,
to the wind's cold syllable.

In the course
of past lives
and preterit disinterments,
I've been a creature of the elements
and keep on being a corpse in the city:
I cannot abide the niche,
prefer woodlands with startled
pigeons, mud, a branch of
chattering parakeets,
the citadel of the condor, captive
of its implacable heights,
the primordial ooze of the ravines
adorned with slipperworts.

Yes yes yes yes yes yes,
I'm an incorrigible birder,
cannot reform my ways—
though the birds
do not invite me
to the treetops,
to the ocean
or the sky,
to their conversation, their banquet,
I invite myself,
watch them
without missing a thing:
yellow-rumped siskins,

dark fishing cormorants
or metallic cowbirds,
nightingales,
vibrant hummingbirds,
quail,
eagles native
to the mountains of Chile,
meadowlarks with pure
and bloody breasts,
wrathful condors
and thrushes,
hovering hawks, hanging from the sky,
finches that taught me their trill,
nectar birds and foragers,
blue velvet and white birds,
birds crowned by foam
or simply dressed in sand,
pensive birds that question
the earth and peck at its secret
or attack the giant's bark
and lay open the wood's heart
or build with straw, clay, and rain
their fragrant love nest
or join thousands of their kind
forming body to body, wing to wing,
a river of unity and movement,
solitary
severe birds among the rocky crags,
ardent, fleeting,
lusty, erotic birds,
inaccessible in the solitude
of snow and mist,
in the hirsute hostility
of windswept wastes,
or gentle gardeners
or robbers
or blue inventors of music
or tacit witnesses of dawn.

A people's poet,
provincial and birder,
I've wandered the world in search of life:
bird by bird I've come to know the earth:
discovered where fire flames aloft:
the expenditure of energy
and my disinterestedness were rewarded,
even though no one paid me for it,
because I received those wings in my soul
and immobility never held me down.